The Scent of Royal Sound

The Scent of Royal Sound

Vuyiswa Nodada

To order additional copies of this book, contact:
Xlibris Corporation
0-800-644-6988
www.xlibrispublishing.co.uk
Orders@xlibrispublishing.co.uk
Or contact the author at: 076 153 0316, vuyiswan@vodamail.co.za
300341

Contents

PART IV—PASSIONS, VIRTUE AND VICES

PART V—TRIBUTE

PART VI—PRAISE AND PRAYERS

FOREWORD

Someone once said that women were never meant to be understood, but loved. It sounds like something that could have been said of an adorable child, or a pet. Such romantic reflections have contributed significantly to the poetic construction of the female subject. While this construction serves the need to be adored, it denudes the female subject of her complexity.

This collection aims to demystify the female subject, foreground the multifarious processes of reflection that inform her varied experiences, and to peel away the infantilising impositions of the patriarchal view of the femme fatale.

Popular representations of the female by the media borrow significantly from patriarchal grammar. At the heart of this grammar is a penchant for the consumption of the female image. This systematic objectification of the female serves to keep her outside of her own experiences. Consequently, authorship thus becomes crucial in reclaiming both her communal and subjective experiences, to place her, as it were, at the centre of her own narrative.

This collection comes from a series of reflections, intra-personal dialogues, triumphs and defeats with questions of womanhood and the black experience. At best, these are intimidating questions of living in a human body. They are more so unsettling when one realises that one lives in a body marked female by the indifferent whims of biology. And that this marking happens to be in a black skin. These demarcations further problematise female identity precisely because they tend to be interpreted as antitheses in the global patriarchal project of political and economic power.

The collective experience of the female subject shares more than it varies. As a result, racial as well as spatial preoccupations have disadvantaged than benefitted projects of reclamation. This collection is an attempt at acknowledging the experiential sorority that binds all women in the womb of womanhood.

By
Xoli Norman

PREFACE

Literary reflections by women are often a response to patriarchal traditions. This tendency, however, limits the female artist not to mine the many facets of femininity. I have been fortunate enough to grow up in an era where the heroes and breadwinners in my life were women (heroines) albeit in a male dominated world. My grandmother, a widow for the greater part of her life, was a poet and a philosopher who was never trained in the schooling system. She was a woman of authority, a diligent Gardner and very industrious. My mother, who was also a widow at the prime age of thirty five, did odd jobs for her school fees since high school until she completed her four years Diploma in Professional Nursing. She is also a woman of authority in her own right. It is women like my grandmother and mother that have hoisted my literary reflections above the myopia of responding, solely, to patriarchal traditions.

I also write from a black experience, spanning both epochs of the present day South Africa and its Socio-Political past. My life has been enriched by experiences gathered from poor-rural areas in the old Transkei, to low-middle class Township life, to a white dominant and international university world, to middle class racially-mixed urban life in Johannesburg and an opportunity to rub shoulders with the aristocratic communities. Standing in this space, a vista of ideas, memories, and longings converge in my mind breeding reflections that would be a great loss if not recorded.

Today's black female-subject is more aware of her significance in the day to day running of the country's events. She is prepared to give more, dream even some more and demand much more. The journey that has led to the shade has been a protracted wearisome walk in the sun; as aptly put by the Nguni people: *"Indlela ebhek' emthunzini iqala elangeni."* The material documented herein attempts to retrace the steps now hidden in the crust of the earth.

The African female subject reflected in this collection is beautiful but scarred, uninhibited yet timid, confident yet confused, loving but harbouring hate, kind to some but cruel to others, forgiving yet still angry.

She is a walking paradox. After reading this anthology you will see how she can be both emancipated but remain enslaved and how her claim to education and enlightenment threatens the loss of precious African values, sadly, that includes uBuntu.

I am all the above. It is my eleven years old daughter, Nelisa, who systematically peels off my maternal layers to reveal these seemingly contradictory states. However, in her I see a different species of the African woman emerging. Her generation is more confident, more ambitious, free thinkers who never cease to amaze me. Almost every day I am fed with a dose of these attributes. At times, she does it in the morning, in the kitchen just before she heads off to school.

"I hate my Drama class and today I am going to tell so and so where to get off." She would complain but justify her case eloquently.

"Nelisa!" I would simply reprimand, dumbfounded.

I am sometimes challenged by such confidence and her readiness to use such strong language, a taboo in my days as a child. In her I see also the long held dream of the black woman turning into a nightmare. Who are we? Who is the Free Black Woman? Who is the African Woman? Where is the Royal African Woman?

Although my biological father was neither a king nor a prince, his mother, Manala, my grandmother, awakened the spiritual princess in me. She was a great story teller. African tales with history and philosophy weaved in, were her specialty. I gleaned from her fair tales that Africa was not ruled by Presidents and Prime Ministers in the olden days but by kings and queens, princes and princesses and chiefs with their wives. Royalty reigned in Africa. Royalty was common. Royalty was revered.

It is told that young women in my clan, although commoners, used to be married by kings because of their startling beauty hence one of my clan names or praises is *Nonkosi* (Nkosi means king). This, I internalised and carried myself out like a Cinderella.

"Nkosazana!" (Princess) is what my grandmother called me citing that in our culture that is the status given to a first born daughter. Whenever she visited my mother's house, she would throw her weight around in making sure that I do not lift a finger. Then she would order people around to serve me, the princess.

As I grew in my spiritual and religious life, I learned that I am in fact royal. Not because a prince kissed me from my deep sleep or I kissed a frog turned prince as told in my favourite fairy tales. If my spiritual father is King and Lord and my spiritual brother is a King of kings that makes me the Princess. That notion emancipates me to a high, noble, royal and lofty plane.

The Scent of Royal Sound is a collection of poetry that attempts to unearth the noble and royal essence of an African woman. It is also an attempt to showcase the strength and tenacity of the African Woman. It also portrays and depicts her beautiful, tender and fragrant side hence I chose the word *'scent'* to depict the influence (as the scent disseminates its fragrance or aroma) she has in building her nation and in advancing her earthly and heavenly kingdom.

Take my hand and come with me, as I unveil the mystery of the African woman's soul. Let me take you through the maze of The Scent of Royal Sound. Listen to the sounds as she groans with pain. Hear the noise as she laughs out loud. Experience her fury and flaws. See her resilience painted through these pages. Come watch her dance. Enjoy her acts of Ubuntu. Come and walk these pages with me as she journeys to reclaim her place in the palace. Listen to the music in her voice as she tells her own story through poetry.

DEDICATION

I dedicate this book, first and foremost, to my mother, Gertrude Nobantu Nodada-Makola, secondly to my daughter, Nelisa.

I also dedicate my work to the love of my life Xoli Norman and his family especially Sma Mkhefe whose support has been the winds beneath our wings.

ACKNOWLEDGEMENT

I would like to thank Professor Mxolisi Leslie Dikeni for making the time to edit this book. I am grateful for the invaluable technical guidance he shared in making this book a reality.

PART I

Essence

1.   *The Scent of Royal Sound*

Her voice thunders
Her chest a storming volcano
Spitting bottled years of silence
Erupting ripples of sound quake

Her cry rages and wages war
Her sound a battle cry:
"Dethrone king Prejudice, dethrone prince Abuse
Enthrone queen uBuntu, enthrone princess Love"

Pregnant with fragrance
Her petals unfold
Scenting the winds with the blood of both the rose and the thorn of her
    days
Spreading like a virus the scent of royal sound

Her noise for emancipation trumpets
Tearing walls of iron cocoon
Birthing a caterpillar with Eagle wings
Flying the scent of royal sound

The scent of royal sound
To the sexist and tribalist—a therapy, a day with daisies and lilies in Khoisan
    land
To the low self-esteemed—a remedy, a smell of earth after the rain in the
    Sahara

To the discerning and wise—a calabash overflowing with lessons and
  experiences

The scent drums the sound
Come dance, come dance, come dance
The scent drums the royal sound
Come reason, come reason, come reason.

2.   *Royalty*

From valley to hill my eyes danced
From the land of the Khoi and the San to the Nile I scouted
Adventure hiked me up Mount Kilimanjaro
My knee almost bent to its majesty

Adrenalin rushed me to the Cango caves
Thriller befriended
Mystic charms soaked my senses
Taming every nerve

The magic broom flew me to Victoria Falls
My soul sailed the rainbow
I sailed to Cape Point, saw the Atlantic and the Indian lashing like Serena
     and Venus
Awe kissed my forehead as Wonder hugged me

My Mpundulu (animal used in witchcraft) galloped to Zanzibar
I felt the crown on my head and the scepter on my right hand
To the Serengeti my head almost bowed
With Thabo Mbeki I roared: "I am an African"

Boom! Before my eyes nobility poised
To this creature my eyes locked
From this being my feet immobilised
A work of art spread before my eyes

Resting on her head a bucket the height of my dish washing machine
Her head garbed with a head gear the size of my dress
Her neck adorned with beads the length of my stiletto
Her face adorned with dots like the art work on my French-acrylic nails
On one hand a bag the weight of my laptop plus portable printing &
     scanning machine
On her back a being the weight of my microwave oven
Under her arm a live hen the size of my food processing machine

Carrying in her heart uBuntu the measure of my ignorance and apathy

I saw a being whose royal spirit beat the awe of Victoria Falls
I saw a royal soul devoid of a throne but devout to serve
Her majesty beat Mount Kilimanjaro
Nobility and dignity crowned her

From the Zulu kingdom, to the Sotho kingdom, to Ethiopia she dazzled
    me the same
From kwaXhosa, to the baTsonga, to Zimbabwe, to Somalia she drummed
    the same heart beat
Across the oceans, over the seas, she struck with the same semblance with
    the daughters of the soil
Where ever I spotted her, she struck me with royal aura

Now I retire under an avocado tree in the kingdom of the baVenda with
    my hand on my chin:

Is it in the clapping of her hands when she laughs?
Is it in the waving of her hands when she worships?
Is it in the swaying of her hips when she dances?
Is it in the bursting out in song when she toils?

Is it in her deep spring of love unquenchable?
Is it in her giving 'till she's naked?
How does she forgive enormity?
How does she put it all behind her, while her wounds are bleeding and
    septic?

Is it in her pride, though raped?
Is it in her content soul, though dispossessed of land in her motherland?
Is it her unrelenting Tsunami bearing to fend for her offspring restitution?
Is it in her resilience to war the glass ceiling?

Is it in the kiss of her thick lips?
Is it in her elevated bosom and cushioned behind?
Is it in her libidinous inferno?
Is it in her voice, the harmony of her unrehearsed symphony?

Maybe it's that the nature and science of uBuntu is her very essence
Maybe it's in her faith in the creator God or in her mystic traditions
Maybe it's in her grip of a God who resembles Black Strength
Maybe her God is black.

3.   *The Royal Phoenix*

The six feet deep pit, deepened her refusal to rot
Though darkness prevailed, light illuminated
Her inner eye diffused the rut
Her princely will summoned sovereign courage to spade a way out
Defying the confines of her box and gravity
She arose

Eyes bulged, hearts raced and lower jaws dropped
Didn't Judas and the Cross Fanatics build her coffin as Noah's ark?
Didn't Ishmael and Israel cast in stone her grave as the Egyptian pyramids?
Didn't the African warrior thrust his spear to her heart as to a buffalo?
Didn't the Eurocentric capitalist steal her kingdom and looted her gold
      and oil?
Eyes bulged, hearts raced and lower jaws dropped

Defying gravity and confines of her box, she arose
From the ashes she arose to chair the Boardroom
From nowhere she arrived to rule in Parliament
From the dusty roads she leaped to Wall Street
From the ghetto to the White House—the first lady
With the Eagles she soars!

4.   *House of Beauty*

What makes the moon shine?
Who gives the stars their twinkle?
What excites the three sisters to dance?
The black curtain
The black velvet screen
My black skin

My black skin is the platter that holds the kings and queens of the galaxy
My black skin is the black diamond tray that holds the kingly Milky Way
My pigmentation is the ink of life that impregnates the white cloud black
For only the black cloud houses life
For only the black cloud houses hope
For only the black cloud is a house of beauty

For as long as I am hungry, I will never see the beauty of white sands
For as long as I am chained, I will never feel the beauty of clay soil
For as long as I reign, on black soil only shall I stretch my kingdom
For trapped in the black soil is wealth, health and prosperity
For the black soil houses fertility
My black skin makes me the house of beauty

PART II

History

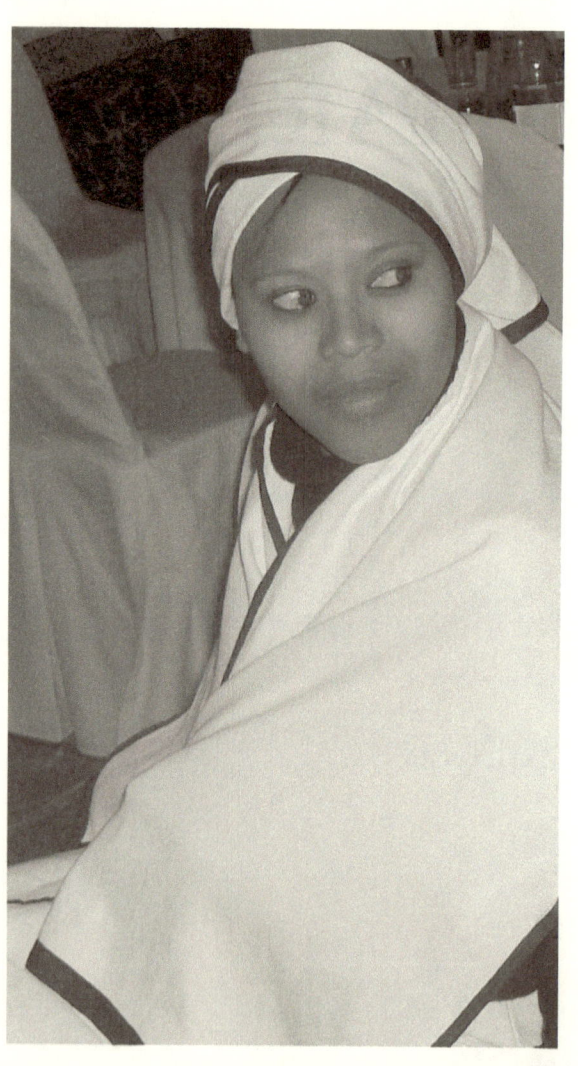

5. *My Grandmother*

Cleaned Madam's cutlery silver new
Polished *Baass'* (boss, master) trophies glory new
Scrubbed *klein baass'* (small boss, young master) toilet odour free
But herself

Cleaned Misis' glasses to crystal clear
Dolled Magda's bedroom to a princess's haven
Dusted Baass' study room to corporate image
But herself

Branded foods to the dogs she fed
Grand meals to the Vervoeds she tabled
Prime years, donkey strength she gave
But her children

Morning, June 16, 1976, she bathed and dressed Magda for school
Morning, June 16, 1976, she walked Mary-Ann to school
Afternoon, June 16, 1976, she carried Mary-Ann's school books and walked
    her home
But her sons and daughters

Evening, June 16, 1976, in warm water she bathed Magda
Evening, June 16, 1976, she kindled the fire place to kick the wintery blanket
Evening, June 16, 1976, she tucked her in and sang her a prayer from
    Ntsikana's hymn
"Ulo Thixo omkhulu, Osezulwini, Unguyena yena ikhakha lenyaniso
Aha ahomna! Ahom hom na! Aha ahomna! Ahom hom na"
(Oh mighty God, the God in heaven, You are the only shield, the shield of
    truth)
But her offspring cold corpses, littered on icy streets

6.   *The Lament*

Sharpeville Day, I'd change your name to Martyr's Day
I'd declare you a day of mourning, a day of lament
Alas, a day of celebration you have become
Alas, like any other day, a "human rights day" you are called

Coin me a word for black on black treachery
Mint me a word for black against black treason
What kind of demon would romanticise genocide?
Unsacred is the spirit that killed Sharpeville day

Only an uncircumcised spirit would dare kill Shaka's day
"Heritage day" waters down black bravery and valour
"Braai Day" buries the remnants of African heritage in *Mzantsi* (South)
    Afrika
This cosmetic surgery hides the scars that remind where we came from

Leave the white skeletons and skulls lying on the streets as monuments
Leave the blood stained skirts and aprons unwashed—to rebuke
Why feed her stories to the dogs?
How will she appreciate her dreams if you wipe out her nightmares?

7. *Reflections*

Sharpeville, I'd change your name to Bluntville, to Brutalville, to Eventville
Your valleys re-birthed David and Goliath
Though on the map Vereeniging in Transvaal is insignificant yet on the
    minds you remain immortal
Your valleys, innocent unarmed men and women massacred

You started small on 13 May 1902 marking the beginning of an end
Anglo-Boer War on exit, ushering in Apartheid
1910 rolled out the foreplay of Exclusive Co-operation
Pseudo freedom enjoyed by English and Afrikaans species only

Eventful 1933, 1948 and 1958 took baby steps to the infamous 1960
United Party, The National Party and the Segregation laws raced towards you
Eventful 1908, 1912 and 1959 also marched for you
Mohandas K. Gandhi's arrest, African National Congress' birth siblinged
    by Pan Africanist Congress progressed towards you

Khaki shorts, khaki socks and red necks you called—Hendrik Verwoerd
    heeded
Khaki shirts, bare feet and yellow teeth you beckoned—Robert Mangaliso
    Sobukwe harkened
Boycotts, mass actions, protests and strikes dared you 1960
State-of-emergency, torture, murder, bans and arrests-without-trial counter-
    acted.

Lest I forget my history, reflections of Sharpeville live on
Reflections of Sharpeville rebuke, unmask the new oppressor
Reflections of Sharpeville deter the new fierce tide of uprisings and senseless
    deaths
Service delivery protests could just be a fore-play.

8. *The Nightmare*

Sharpeville you were not the only battlefield
A cry of "*Amandla nga wethu*" (power is ours) transcended from Langa and
    Gugulethu in Cape Town
The shouts of "*Mayibuye i Afrika*" (Africa must return) thundered from
    Kwa Mashu and Umlazi in Kwa Zulu Natal
Johannesburg's Soweto simply echoed "one settler one bullet", "*leth'umshini
wam*" (bring my machine gun)

Vanderbijlpark also felt the pinch
Bophelong offered death than life
Boibatong was also blood stained
Everton not spared

But you oh Sharpeville, you sharpened your double edged sword
The ANC's planned march was too far for you, so you back stabbed
You rushed in the radicals. "Africa for Africans", chanted the PAC
The ANC's plans you disturbed

Five thousand protestors amassed your grounds with a dream
Three hundred remained to claim the dream and faced the music
Dream turned to nightmare for the one hundred and eighty maimed survivors
The nightmare left sixty-nine scattered brains trashed on the African soil

How does one Earthling turn another Earthling's dream to a nightmare?
What amount of hate would aggravate another man's nightmare to hell?
Bullets chasing to injure nineteen children and thirty one women in one
 hour! What hell?
Bullets chasing to kill eight women and ten children in an hour! What
 senseless hostility?

Uninvited, the African woman partnered with men and lived the nightmare
Uninvited, the Black woman did not remain in the kitchen, but faced brutality
The nightmare did not, could not scare the valiant African woman away
The Black Woman martyred paying the price for your dream.

Her nightmare a ransom, a great price that redeemed your dream
Her cold, long, dark night purchased your dawn
Now walk tall, take your place with the queens and kings, the
philosophers, judges, and bishops
Go to the moon, discover a new planet
Live the dream

9. *Valour*

If Helen Joseph could stare death in the eye
If Bertha Gxowa could poke the demon's eye
If Lilian Ngoyi could prod anger
Why then should I be silent when BEE Tenderpreneur mongers rob the
    hungry?

If the day's comforts did not attract Violet Hedburg
If Amina Cachalia forsook her automobile to walk the talk
If Rahima Moosa gave to the hungry her last Samoosas
Why then should I be silent when greedy school officials loot the feeding
    scheme?

If Lizzie Diedricks sacrificed her time
If Sophy Williams De Bruyn sacrificed her career
If Albertina Sisulu sacrificed her family
How do I continue to amass, accumulate and live for self?

Oh women of virtue, Black and White, Indian and Coloured, arise and rebuke
Felicia Mabuza Suttle come revive the ambitions, empathy and self-worth
Winnie Madikizela Mandela come remind that unity is power
Black Sash, from your wells of experience, exhibit how to reprimand your
    own

How can I be silent when my fetus is butchered to be fed to fat cats?
How can I keep quiet when moral degeneration is regenerating?

Oh woman of valour, refuse to die, for an endangered species you are
Revive your *uBuntu* (humanitarian spirit)
Remember *inimba* (labour pains and empathy)
Remember *uQamata* (your God).

10.   *Her Story*

Who could stop *abafazi* (women) in unity?
Who could discourage *abafazi* (women) with one mission?
Who could diffuse their unified vision?
Show me one man who stood against them

Success spectacular!
Force phenomenal!
Ability beyond male comprehension!
Capability above Native Commissioner's imagination

Pretoria, Union Buildings: The initial destination
Abolished Pass laws: The short term goal
Boundary-less South Africa: The vision
To free minds plagued with racial divisions: The mission

How do four queen bees hum over twenty thousand women?
How do you harmonise an unrehearsed symphony of different races, ages
    and classes?
In unison they sang
In unison they sang

Helen Joseph staged countrywide road shows, six weeks prior to D-day
Bertha Gxowa rallied around her comrades singing unity is strength
Lilian Ngoyi motivated and mobilized the women masses, paving the way
    to D-day
Yes tell her story in boring detail as you would tell his story

In Potchefstroom she protested against the Poll Tax, who said she wasn't
aware of Fiscal and Monetary Policies?
In Natal, she turned white man's beer tables upside down, who said she
wasn't a catalyst for Socio-Political changes?
In the Western Cape she protested against increasing food prices, who said
she was not conversant with Macro Economics?

Yes tell her story in boring detail as you would his story
In 1950 she fought against Bantu Education
In 1952 she ushered in The Freedom Charter
In 1952 she rallied behind The Defiance Campaign
In 1953 she drafted The Women's Charter

Her story records: On 9 August 1956 she delivered petition to Prime
Minister JG Strijdom
Her story records: In 1955, Black Sash, the white sisters, marched to the
lion's den in Pretoria
Oh tell her story over and over again
Tell her story in boring detail, as you would tell his story.

12. *One Thing Left*

On the alters of lust my remains lie
To the unquenched fires of passion I'm the sacrificed
I give of myself to the ungiving
Desecrating the consecrated

My heart is slain with each stroke,
My essence crushed with each groan of pleasure
They jerk and joke: "The lady of the night". They ask how much?
How much is dignity loss? What's the price for lost integrity? I ask

Oh that my soul may not be party to this transaction
Oh that I may not trade my spirit
For that's all left to protect
My spirit, the only thing not raped off me.

13.   *Ghosts*

(Dedicated to the 16 days of Activism in South Africa against children and women)

Ghosts frighten me every day I walk the streets of Johannesburg.
They follow me like a bird of prey. I see a bird fly I dive and hide. Paranoia has become my friend.

Ghosts laugh at me on my face mocking: where's the freedom? Where's safety and security? I am imprisoned, living behind boom gates, high walls and electric-fences. Yet I am exposed, left to fend for myself in a neglected squatter camp. Yet I'm vulnerable, though only fourteen, forced to mother others.

The cry of a raped nine month old baby won't be hushed in my dreams. The gun shots that claimed a baby secure on his mother's back trigger nightmares.

The Ghost of drug abuse raped and mugged my grandmother for her pension pennies. Her stench from the cocktail of urine, semen and blood mortify my femininity.

The Ghost of greed robbed my family a breadwinner ushering in the ghost of hunger, poverty and prostitution.

The Ghosts of violence ganged up to gang-rape my sister. Ghosts of crime came to hijack, smash and grab leaving me shaking like a leaf. Leaving me hopeless and helpless in my own motherland. I envy my European neighbour who boarded the next brain-drain train.

These ghosts haunt and scare the living daylights out of me. They hunt me like I'm the last prey. Though spirits of the lowest abyss—I saw their faces. Ostracise and apprehend these ugly things.

14. *Queen Nandi's Daughter*

Like a bird that lost her nest, she hovered
She wouldn't stop pointing at nothing
Like a hen robbed of her eggs from its nest, she kept on searching the debris
Mumbling something about fire, shack, ashes and lost trading stock

Like a chicken scratching the grass in search for grains
She inspected for hours on end the ashes in search of anything to salvage
Exhausted, dirty, wet with sweat, stinking, hungry and thirsty
She sat on the ashes, and wept: I remember palace

Which dark powers transformed this princess to a popper?
Which portion displaced her from palace to no-place?
How did she cascade from riches to rags?
Who stole the Bread Basket of Africa?

15. *Boomerang*

Go ahead sneer but smear me not
Go ahead jest but I suggest judge me not
For your forefather schooled me not
For your father skilled me not

Now you judge: "incompetent"
But your nephew will not share skills endowed down to him
Now you sentence: "ineffective"
But your brother is not bothered with human capital development

Skills transfer train you will not board, brain drainage plane you boarded
But with my lacking service you are bored
Black Economic Empowerment train you will not board
But with my unempowered delivery you are bored

16. *Loosing Adam*

Once upon a time, time would cease to exist, while in his embrace
Once upon a time, time was lost in his kiss
All at once, time is eternity without his presence
All at once, alone, I must face the music; alone I must do the tango

With one hand I am left to handle the fruits of our love union
With one hand I am left to mend a thousand gaps, to feed many a hungry
     tummy
With a blur vision I am left to navigate, map, direct, compass and steer to
     shore
With one leg I must run the race

17. *The Eternal Lament*

There exists a forlorn specimen
There exists a problem no Einstein, nor Dr Freud, nor modern technology
    can resolve
Science refuted the claims but acknowledged the facts
There exists a strange product of two: a fatherless child

Where is the good black man?
Is he only jammed in a few good black men?
Is he only boxed in Hollywood's tall, dark and handsome?
Does he only feature in Falsehood?

Biology please explain to me "fatherless"
Not even the animal kingdom suffer from such a scourge
A search for a God fearing black man with integrity is on. Will my neighbor
    feature?
The search is on for a black family man who maintains not a weakness to
    love only his wife

When you find him hide him. He's black brother Cain thirsts for his blood
God forbid it that he will be but a figment of the next generation's imagination
His absence on the dinner table, at the church pew, at the parent's meeting,
    is Polio that cripples many a brilliant child
His presence at the drinking place, the gambling place and at the mistress'
    home is but death to many diligent home makers and nation builders.

18. *Waste*

Your sons and daughters are of no value
The future of your children is of no consequence
Community building is of no use
Scorns the scale of the Drug Dealer: only money weighs

Your mother's tears—not the drug lord's fear
Your father's anger—not the drug lord's danger
Your son's soul—his gold
Your daughter's blood—his booty

Home traded for a bench in the park and dinner for dust bin: a small fee
    for a high
You don't think so? Go ask a Junkie

Alas the littered talent
Alas brains down the drain
Albeit without measure
Apprehend substance abuse. Lock the dealer and the drug Lord and throw
    away the key.

19.   *The Enemy*

In memory of Patricia Nodada

The venom struck again
The predator hit again
A fraction added to the ever escalating statistics
A fragile frame added to the ever hungry abyss

This time at my door step
This time around, a dear sister
A daughter
A mother

ABCs?
Where do babies come from?
Taboo topics?
Pronounce! Proclaim! Preach! Teach!

Sex: God's gift to mankind for marital recreation and procreation
Sex misused: the devils weapon of mass destruction
Sex: a moment's pleasure
Sex abused: a memory's torture

How many orphans must be mass produced? Before we harken
How many desolate, broken homes? Before we heed
How many street kids? Before we reckon
How many law breakers? Before we feel

Cursed art thou, HI Virus and AIDS, oh you cruel monster!
Despised are you, oh you merciless demon!
You disgust you obnoxious butcher!
You repulse you greedy beast, sly serpent!

Abstain! Shout it aloud you Christians
Abstain! Echo it you Muslims
Be faithful to your partner—strengthen moral regeneration
Be faithful to your partner—deprive moral degeneration

Condomise, put on those gloves, change that needle
Conduct appeals, be sober minded
Conduct beckons wisdom
Conduct calls to repentance

Conduct rooted in old African values, begs
Conduct ordained by old Christian principles, appeals
Conduct ready to restore us to *Ubuntu bethu* (our humanity) pleads
Embrace conduct, the better way.

20. *Death Lives*

’Tis sunset
Fears set
The moon shines
The mood changes

Evening’s dark shadows creep
I must cry myself to sleep
Time to endure the long hours to follow
Time to face the hollow pillow

Sleep, my sweet relief
Dreams, my good release
There he is, full of life
A hug, a kiss, I give

The feeling so great and beautiful
The place so green and bountiful
He lives
Love breaths

We walk
We talk
We chase
We engage

My time is up, he says
I must leave, he begs
No! We have eternity, I say
No! Do not leave I pray

A warm embrace
A long gaze
Slowly he moves away
Faster he brisks, still facing my way

Backward strides, gain pace
Walking turns to running
Running turns to gliding, then to flying into space
In disbelief I watch him disappear

Dream so sweet!
Dreaded nightmare?
Sleep so deep!
Sorrow beyond compare?

The morning bird sings
My lonely heart sinks
Reality strikes
Death lives

Killing so senseless
Death so cruel
Killing so careless
Death so brutal

Life traded for a wallet, a car, a cell phone?
Life for a thing, what a senseless exchange?
Hope dies, crime thrives
Death lives.

21. *How Long?*

What system can ever repair the damage?
What compensation can ever restore her stolen inheritance?
Affirmative action can only begin
Black Economic Empowerment is only a drop in the ocean

For how long will social grants pacify her needs?
Who really understands her needs and desires?
One Act amendment bill after another will still not amend
Would a million gold mines quench her dry soul?

For as long her arch enemy continues to breathe
For as long her seed continues to crush his head
For as long his seed continues to crush the heel of her offspring
Her soul cannot rest; she will drink but thirst again, but for how long?

For as long as she possesses the beauty and displays the splendor the enemy
        lost
For as long as she creates life
For as long as the serpent finds men and women it can use against her
Her soul cannot rest, but for how long?

For how long will the tears flow her tender cheeks?
For how long will she sleep on a hungry stomach in a land of plenty?
When will her ship arrive? When will she rest? When will her labour cease?
When will she see the advent of the second coming?

PART IV

Passions, Virtue and Vices

22.   *Brown Woman to Brown Woman*

You spit venom at your own eyes, worse than a snake you've become
Hate blinds you that your eyes see outlaws and in-laws the same
Hate deafens you that you won't step in when a step child cries
An arch enemy to yourself you've become, allowing her husband to your
    bosom

Chains of slavery on your subjects you yoke
You table a table of exploitation and abuse to the one who tables your
    table
One degree decrees you choice grade and others no grade
Behind the counter and computer, behind the apron, behind the till you
    diss your own

With twisted love you raise a black Cain
With rations of superiority, irresponsibility and indulgence you feed your
    boy child
With an iron hand you rear up the weaker vessel
With loose morals you nurture the future head of the home

Why cry foul when the chicken come to roost?
Poof! On your face it will surely blow!
Turn off the TV; come watch the vicious cycle as it plays out.
Oh no, do not weep, for this is your sowing you are reaping.

23. *Miss Qonda*

Click, click, click, to the black board the red high-heels halted
Like music, the fragrance filled the classroom
The Naomi Campbell silhouette got all eyes facing the front
Like sunflowers in dawn, ears, hearts, minds and spirits opened up

She was not necessarily the prettiest
Knowing who she was made her the loveliest
She was not necessarily the wisest
Knowing whose she was and where she came from made her the smartest

Girls like me, wouldn't dare ask Miss Mirror how they fare
Girls like me, hated a part or everything about themselves
Girls like me, like a tortoise, lived more in their shells
Girls like that, made her cry

She taught: "You are packaged in a unique way for a different purpose in life"
She negated: "There is no such thing as an ugly woman"
She reminded: "You all have the same mother, Eve. Each one will resemble
　　some of her original untainted beauty.
She reminded: You are all flawed in some way. Each one of you will exhibit
　　sin marks be it stretch marks, big eyes or small eyes.
With tears in her eyes she repeated: "You still bear the beauty of the original,
　　no matter how marred
With a lump in her throat she whispered: You are endowed of Eden's origi-
　　nal beauty, no matter how tainted

Today she still flaunts a bling that beats my Guess and Louis-Vuitton accessories
Today she exudes a flare that beats my Gucci and Levis` items
Today she still wears a smile that beats my Este`e Lauder facial treatment
　　and make-up
Her wisdom, inner-peace and inner-beauty brighten a brilliant brow that
　　never wears up.

24. *Drum It*

Beat it! *Shaya! Betha! Betsa!*
Drum the drum. *Letsa moropa olle*
Gudum, gudum, gudu gudu gudum
Drum it to the rhythm of my heart

Beat it fast when I sing of Shaka, Biko and Mandela
Beat it faster when I sing of my husband
Drum it to my pulse, the rhythm of our love
Drum it steady for the *abakwetha* (boys in initiation school) when they
    come home

Drum it louder for the wedding
Halala! Halala! Halala! Yehaaaa! Lili-lili!
Swirl and shake your *Xibelani* (skirt) you Tsonga girl
Let your feet drum the ground you Zulu girl

Drum it slowly as you sing your king's praises you Venda girl
        Mavu!
        Tshivhavhala tsha shango,
        Mthombeni,
        Maila u sumbwa,
        Lutiitii lwo ambara dzhasi
        Muhali
        Thavha khulu!

Halala, halala, lili-lili, yehaa!
Ululate louder you Xhosa girl
Drum it as you dance around the fire
Drum it for mother earth as she dances around the globe
....

25. *The Dragon Fly*

Your beak forever nectars from hidden sewages
Your mouth forever fishing worms from buried carcass
Bees and butterflies fly away from faeces and white pass, you see a feast
You dragon! In hell you will fry

Your wings find pleasure in spreading malice
Your tongue though invisible, invincible broken hearts you boast
Broken homes and split churches you boast
You dragon! In heaven you will not fly.

26. *Dear Diary*

Don't want no white face on my face
Aint fillin them cold blank lines
With me, it gotta be face to face
Better still over the fence

Don't want no white face on my face
Aint gonna spill black blood on them white lines
Damn page won't say: "It will be alright, hang in there"
Dumb page won't cry with me.

27.   *Go Green*

See the Princess of the night, steady with grace, walking to her palace
No matter how slow, she never misses her train
Hear the Prince from the land with white valleys and white hills galloping
No matter how anxious with the chill he brings, he never arrives before time
No matter how stubborn her children, Mother Nature must be obeyed

When she says take care of your body in youth for it will take care of you
     in old age—you better heed
When she says drink water, exercise, eat green—you better harken
When she says take care of your environment for it will take care of
     you—listen
Each new green shrub planted, keeps her wrath away.

28. *Mama*

No Goldsmith can produce a finer gold than you
No Jeweler can craft a finer pearl than you
Your mines of generosity and sacrifice are inexhaustible
Your wells of love and wisdom unquenchable

No words could ever be worthy enough to thank you enough
No praises could ever be powerful enough
When it comes to thanking you Mama, this Poet is dumbfound
I can only lisp 'Thank you Mama'
I can only stammer *Mandaba, Bhadela, Tshibase!* (Praise song about her
    clan name)

29. *The Love Bug*

Day dreams order my day
Smiles tracking from ear to ear attack my face
I'm all aglow, singing a song whose words I long forgot

First date sent invading visions of babies, of Junior playing with Daddy at
    the park
One kiss flowered visions of the 'I dos, you may kiss the bride'
But who is he? Where is he from?

Nocturnal dreams denied, home alone, I twist and turn
In my dreams I see him filling the rest of the pages of my life's story
But who is he?

30. *Interrogation Room*

Didn't I shut that door?
Didn't I lock and threw the key away?
I know it was barred, chained, razor wired
This is burglary, help! He's come to steal my heart away

Didn't I prohibit "NO ENTRY"?
I know I repelled—"Right of admission reserved"
Didn't I repulse "Enter at own risk"?
I know I scared "Trespassers will be prosecuted"

My world shaken
My grip threatened
World spinning under my feet
With the clouds I float

What force is this, which defies gravity?
Who is this master conjurer, what laws at play?
The push and the pull war for me
Faith and sight war in me

To let go or not to let go is the question
To let loose? To take the leap?
To let be?
To jump or not to jump is the question

Honesty weigh him, will he score?
Integrity interrogate him, will he fare?
For my heart will he care?
For true love will he dare? Will he sacrifice? Will he forsake all others?

31. *Pride*

Though a breed often labeled and mocked
My price tag is diamonds and pearls
My heart pumps in freedom from worry and pumps out bright future
Each new moon showers with medals of innocence and crowns of beauty

Like a closed budded rose before its bloom so is my womanhood
Like a honey comb soaked in nectar so is my manhood
After-party begged to mine a little of my gold, I yelled NO
Curiosity invited, but saying YES to the Royal Call, I said NO

The Twenty-First Key begged
Curiosity screamed
I whispered NO
For only the RING or the LOBOLA is the right key to my sealed pleasure
    treasure

32. *Between The Sheets*

Scoop away the stars, blot the galaxies and erase the firmament, the day he
    walks away
Suck the oceans dry, let the vacuum show
Expose the expanse, for that is my heart empty of him.

Suspended in space between heavens, beauty above allures and beauty
    below beckons
White sheets dancing lazily fill my view but my mind escapes it all
My untamed spirit flew out the windows of my soul and escaped the bird
Hunted him down, brought him to the chambers, his palace

Me and him between the sheets, keep me there forever and ever
Give this bird a mission to fly around the world
Like the Apollo reaching the peak, the top sheet is torn apart and dumped
    below
The pleasure consumes my very being
Ecstasy caresses my every nerve, massaging each fiber, theraping each cell.

33. *M.B.A. Man*

He'll open the car for you
He'll send you flowers
He'll call from work
He'll never be late
Alas! He is an M.B.A man.
Married But Available
He holds Honours and Masters degree in serial heart breaking and home
     wreckage
Run away
Stay away.

PART V

Tribute

34. *The Fall*

A Tribute to the late Mama Miriam Zenzile Makeba also known as Mama Afrika

The Earth pulled her night blanket over her eyes refusing to see "The Fall"
The Sun went to sleep refusing to witness "The Fall"
Mother Africa sent her on an errand to Europe; she could not bear "The Fall"
Mother Earth's telecom-lines clogged, heralding to all her habitats: "The
    Fall", "The Fall"

As in paving the way for a Princess
The sons of the soil went ahead
In rapid succession they followed each other
Lucky Dube, Jabu Khanyile, Vuyo Mokoena

As in paving the way for a Queen
The sons and daughters of the soil went ahead
The nation was still in mourning robes for her beloved Ma Nokwe
The nation was still in shock, in denial, Eskia Mpahlele can't be gone

Yes many bear babies but a few heed to the calling of motherhood
It takes immeasurable pain, tears and endurance to earn the title "Mama"
To earn the title "Mama Afrika" takes far reaching self sacrifice and self denial
To earn the title "Mama Afrika" one must be garbed by the garment of Ubuntu

Though your branches spread far beyond Africa
Yet your roots remained anchored in the belly of the mother land, Africa
You shone in King Kong and twinkled in Come Back Africa
You illuminated Graceland and flavoured Sarafina

Scooped Grammy awards! What a role model
Snatched the Dag Hammarskjold Peace Prize! What an ambassador
Shared the Polar Music Prize! Earned the Gold Otto Hahn Peace Medal!
No wonder wonderful Nelson Rolihlahla Mandela, in 1990 beckoned you
     back home

What consolation can suffice?
What could wipe away the tears of the nation?
For this tree sheltered many a weary souls
For this tree orcharded many a hungry stomachs.

35. *Lend Me a Day*

In memory of my sister the late Neliswa Nodada who died young, in a car accident.

Like the forgiven Mary Magdalene, who went away with murder
I'd stick with Him
I'd spend on Him
Love Him and live for Him
Only if you could lend me a day

Like the Samaritan woman after her encounter at the well
I'd go crazy telling my story
See, I've found Christ
Adultery, fornication, sinning, all history
See, I've found life abundant, an oasis

Like the golden and gorgeous queen Esther
I'd put my act together as the day demands
I'd fast and pray as the time so demands
I'd rise up to the high call
I'd influence the great and small
Only if you could lend me a day

Like the pagan Canaanite Mother
I'd nag Him
Till He delivers me from my pleasurable and yet lethal habits
I'd never let go
Till a blessing He throws, till some mercy He drops

Like that merry Miriam
I'd break out loud singing
I'd dance like no one is watching
I'd praise like I just don't care
I'd sing a song that will never ever end

Only if you could lend me a day

36. *One Too Many*

Tribute of the Late Doctor Willie Nodada Msimanga

Blood, tears and sweat secured the trail tailing his name
Diligence, generosity, charm and intellect packaged in one individual, what
    a rare soul!
A lamp-stand and light in the night to many
A death of but one lamp stand in Africa is but one too many

Oh life you are so unpredictable
Twists and turns you present
Good times, exciting times and sad moments alike
Presenting new presidents, new orders, crashing world economies and
    booms alike
Right now we wonder what's next and who is next?

Oh that we may grasp the hand of Him who holds the future
Oh that we may surrender our lives to the One who is the life giver
Like the thief on the cross, see the good doctor on that hospital bed
See him gasping and grasping His hand
See him conversing and confessing
See him surrender his last breath to the One who gave it

See the Saviour saving the one who lived to save and heal his Africa
What a great loss to the African nation in need of rare skills
The African continent mourns but one death of a healer
For one death of a doctor in this disease plagued land is but too many

PART VI

Praise and Prayers

37. *A Shower for a Tear*

When I looked down—misery confronted
When I looked forward—hopelessness jeered
When I searched the end of the tunnel—bleak and darkness mocked,
    inviting the demon of fear
When I looked around, the demon of doubt encamped

Then El Shaddai—the Almighty God
Wrapped His strong arms around me
Lifted my chin up
Wiped that tear away and whispered: "This too shall pass"

Then El Roi—the God who sees me
Responded and reminded: "Trials and tribulations may last but for a night
But Joy, but Joy MUST come in the morning"

Then El Hoseem—the God of Creation
Thundered: "Behold no weapon forged against you will prevail"
He reminded: "Though the mountains be shaken and the hills be removed
    yet my unfailing love for you will not be shaken nor my covenant of
    peace be removed says the Lord who has compassion on you"
The long, dark and cold night gave way to the warm rays of the dawn
    ushered in by the Sun of Righteousness, the Bright Morning Star!

Jehova Jireh never failed to provide
Jehovah Shalom hushed peace in the midst of my storm
Jehovah Nissi, Michael! Mighty at war victored over all my foes
Jehovah Rohi shepherded over me

For every tear drop
A blessing He dropped
For every anguish
Relief He relinquished

My tear drops
Ushered in showers of blessings
Your justice Oh Lord, recompensed beyond comprehension
Your wise comforting words, God the Holy Spirit—I cannot fathom
Your righteousness, supremeness & holiness—too high, too lofty yet you
    remained to me a very nigh God, a Father who is always there for me

Jesus you remained Emanuel—God with me
Yes Emanuel! God with me. God in me!

38. *This African at the Alter I*

Many millenniums ago Africa provided your son Jesus Christ a haven of rest.
Emanuel, God with us, found a safe hiding place from Herod in Africa.
It was safe.
Africa was safe.

An African, Simon of Cyrene, from North Africa, helped Jesus carry His cross.
Africans did not only enjoy good health and great physical strength but
    also deep compassion and empathy.
Compassion shone on Simon's eyes hence the Roman soldiers picked him.
Africa had Ubuntu.
Africa offered help.

Lord we confess we have lost Ubuntu.
Restore in us Your image and we shall naturally bear this fruit of Your Spirit.
We confess our hearts do not feel any more, the devil has benumbed our senses,
    he uses the television as a weapon of mass destruction and we fall prey.
We pray for the Holy Spirit to hover over Africa and regenerate our hearts.

Restore in us our humane nature, we pray Lord!
Restore the African spirit!
Reclaim us.

39.   *This African at the Alter II*

Many centuries ago Africa was a lab and a hub for Civilisation.
We remember Egypt and the hieroglyphics
We remember farming innovations, irrigation schemes that were born
    along the Nile.

Africa was diligent, not lazy.
Africa had great minds, great thinkers.
Africa was a leader.

Oh Lord what went wrong?
Did we leave Your ways and neglected Your Word?
We repent.
Bring back the glory!

Africa pioneered Architecture, Engineering and city building.
We remember Babylon, in Mesopotamia, a world wonder in its times
Africa was building not destroying.
Africa was creative and industrious.
Africa was a pioneer.

Resurrect our ingenious minds we pray Lord!
Help us to build each other up.
Help us to see our own goods and products as good enough.
Help us to support Africa, help us to spend on Africa
When we don't have enough we spend on Chinese and Indian products
When we have enough we spend on Paris, London and New York
Rid us our disease of despising our own, open our eyes.

40. *This African at the Alter III*

Many years ago Africa had the strongest men in the whole wide world.
We remember Nimrod the mighty hunter on the face of the earth.
The best in the world!
Africa had trophies.

Today they learn from big books that a good leader delegates.
Today they speak of, hierarchy, management, division of labour and the likes.
All born of a Cushite mind: Jethro the Priest, Moses' father in law.
Lord didn't you slap Mirriam with leprosy when she spoke ill of a Cushite?
Today, they still call us names.

Lord restore Your image in us.
Help us to surrender our lives to you.
Help us to order our lives according to Your will.
Help us to remember that we are Yours by creation and by redemption.

Once we are in You, You have promised that:
> **You will deal with our enemies and our oppressors**
> **We will be the head not the tail**
> **We shall lend out and never borrow**
> **You shall bless the work of our hands**

Once we abide in You, You have also promised that we will be the apple
of Your eye and no one will touch us.
Lord we believe it.
We claim it!

41.   *This African at the Alter IV*

Once upon a time African daughters resided on thrones
They were given in marriage to kings and princes
The queen of Sheba is but one record.
Ruling and living in opulence and affluence.

Once upon a time Ethiopia was rich and wealthy, with strong armies
Once upon a time Ethiopia had majestic Queens
Once upon a time Ethiopians sought after Your Word,
Phillip's encounter, the disciple of Jesus, is but one record

Could it be that we have forsaken your commandments?
Could it be that we have turned our backs on your statutes?
Could it be that we forgot who is the real source and sustainer of our lives?
Could the curse be in the rejection of your word, the scriptures, the Holy
    Bible?

It's all dark around us now.
We need back the light.
Our lands are plagued with blood shedding and greed.
Power mongering stalks the land
Clouds of poverty, pandemics and pestilence hover on our land

Africa is not the same
Africa is suffering
Lord heal our land and bring back the glory!
Heal our kingdoms and governments
Rekindle the royal vision in our leaders.

42. *This African at the Alter V*

Like fuel on fire, a force from the West poured in
Wolves in sheep's skin invaded our shores
They abused their mission
Misused their position to steal, divide and subdue

Instead of teaching life abundance from Your Word, they stole in abundance
Instead of teaching "thou shall not steal" they looted
Instead of teaching "thou shall not kill" they murdered
Instead of teaching "thou shall have no other gods before me", they
    demanded worship

They labeled Africa "cursed"
They misquoted the account of Noah and his sons to suit their propaganda
We read the account as detailed in Genesis chapters 9 and 10 and we smiled
We read Ham begot Cush and Cush begot Nimrod, a mighty warrior and
    a builder of cities with kingdoms, in Noah's time. Yes the dark-skinned
    ones prospered.
We read the account and learned that Canaan, the last born of Ham was the
    cursed one, and those families were dispersed, for Your Word does not lie.
But Lord even so, the curse did not come from Your mouth but from a
    mere mortal, Noah.

Skepticism, suspicion and rejection of your Holy word, the Bible, resulted.
Superstition and Atheism followed.
Other gods remained worshiped.
Ancestral worship continued.
To images, to carved idols, to the dead, to money, we continued to bow.

But You did not only send the White man to reveal your Holy book, the Bible
You sent many Black prophets and Black priests
Ntsikana, the Xhosa prophet, is but one record
Even today you still use all kinds of people sending them to the ends of
    the earth.
For this gospel is for all mankind, in all the corners of the Earth.
But some missionaries and prophets yield to greed and evil inclinations.
But some endure hardships, the harsh exile lifestyle and they sacrifice their
    very lives.
Good and evil will always war in all human beings whether black, white,
    red or yellow.

Lord this is not the Africa you created,
This is not the Africa of yester years
We know you love Africa,
Africa holds a special place in your heart
We know you have a blessing for Africa
It was you oh God who plagued Miriam, Moses' sister, with leprosy
No one speaks like that about a Cushite, an African and remains unscathed,

We come back to you, please embrace us back to your fold
We claim your promises in 2 Chronicles 7:14

> *"If My people who are called by my name will humble themselves,
> and pray and seek My face, and turn from their wicked ways, **then
> I will hear from heaven, and will forgive their sin and heal
> their land.**"*

Lord heal our land and bring back the glory!

43. *This Princess before the Throne*

Until I defy gravity
Until I dress divinity
Until I inherit eternity
May the Holy Sabbath Oasis download a fore taste of Your kingdom
May the Holy Sabbath Oasis flow springs of blessings and a Pentecost of sanctification
May I continue to say: "For Thine is the kingdom, the power and the glory"

Until I wing through Orion
Until I rule Mars, Pluto and Venus
Until I reign with a golden crown and gold under my feet
May peace, joy and happiness reign in my heart
May wealth, health and beauty reside in my territory
May generosity, forgiveness and healing be readily extended to my subjects

Until I bite from the tree of life
Until I sip from the crystal river of life
Until this mortal royalty kisses immortality and divinity
May the royal incense in my words ascend to scent Your throne
May the royal beat of The Scent of Royal Sound ascend to drum You praises
May The Scent of Royal Sound humble and keep this princess before Your throne.

www.ingramcontent.com/pod-product-compliance
Lightning Source LLC
Chambersburg PA
CBHW020347290526
45785CB00005B/2179